Laugh out Loud!
Pregnancy
By Sharon Irish

Laugh out Loud! Pregnancy

Copyright: Sharon Irish
ISBN: 978-0-9926375-6-9
Published: 15.07.2013
Publisher: Sharon Irish
Cover by: Sharon Irish

Firstly, a little bit about this book:-

When I was pregnant for the first time, I loved reading the magazines for pregnant Mums or Mums with babies as I thought they would prepare me for motherhood (oh how naïve I was!).
I noticed that some of these magazines had a section for funny stories that readers had written in with, but there were only a few of them in each issue. I loved reading them so much, when I was having a bad day (and trust me there were many!) they really cheered me up and I would have happily bought a book full of funny stories from other Women in my position, to make me laugh and help keep me sane!

The stories in this book have been told by *real* Women who have been willing to share their mishaps and embarrassments for the enjoyment of others.

I really hope you enjoy reading this book, and these stories give you something to giggle at, maybe even laugh out loud!

Sharon Irish

Laugh Out Loud!
Pregnancy

Pregnancy/Baby Brain and Hormones:-

Every Woman knows that pregnancy is tough on your body, but it's also tough on your mind! Those hormones rushing through us have a lot to answer for. We drop things and forget things. We're laughing one minute and crying the next, sometimes we know why, sometimes we have no idea!
Here are some examples of just what I mean:-

I walked into my hair salon and said "Hi I'm booked in for a blow job at 11." Obviously I meant to say "blow dry." I've changed Hairdressers since as I can't stand the embarrassment! It was something they would remind me of whenever I went back and the story would be told to all the clients in there at the time.
Emma, UK

It was a really hot night a few weeks ago, I'd got out of the shower and put PJ bottoms on when I went to lock up the front door for the night. Because it was hot I just opened the door and stepped outside onto my front drive

to try and cool down for a minute or two. It was only when I went back in and started talking to hubby that I realised I'd got no top on! I must have given all of our nosey neighbours a shock! I'm normally a very private person so goodness knows what I was thinking!!
Claire, UK

I've done a few daft things recently which I blame on 'baby brain.' One being after my Dad dropped me home one night I thought I had lost my phone and searched my bag for it. A few minutes later I phoned my Dad (using the lost phone, which had been in my hand the whole time), asking if I had left my phone in his car! His silence was deafening!
Ruth, UK

I was at my Mother in Law's house and I couldn't find my phone anywhere. I stole my Husband's phone to call mine and I heard it ring by the dining table so I ran to that area, then it rang again and it sounded like it was near the TV area, so I turned around and looked around there. It rang again and then I swore the sound was behind me! Then I felt my butt vibrate. It was in my back pocket as usual. Mother in Law just stared at me as she watched the whole thing. Good thing I like my Mother in Law!
Becky, USA

I went to straighten my hair but took the clothes iron out of the cupboard and plugged it in before I realised it wasn't my straighteners! Last night I gave my other half a slice of buttered bread for dinner and left his plate of

dinner in the kitchen! He thought I was rationing his food intake! I also, for the life of me, couldn't count out the money at my corner shop for the things I had bought, I had to stand there like a child and just give the Man all my money and let him count out what he needed and give me the rest back! I was so embarrassed especially as there was a queue behind me and everything!
Gemma, UK

I have had a few occasions of 'baby brain.' They mostly involve the fridge for some reason. The first one was when I was making a cup of tea and I put the tea in the fridge instead of the milk. I didn't realise until I went to sit down with a pint of milk! Also once I was cleaning the house and instead of putting my Doppler in a cupboard I went to put it in the fridge until my Husband re-directed me out of the kitchen. Ha Ha!
Maria, UK

One day I couldn't find my favourite sandals anywhere, that night Hubby went to get ice-cream and there they were, in the freezer!
The most stupid thing I've done so far was driving back home from work, sat at the traffic lights and I started to panic, I couldn't find my car key.........in the ignition perhaps!
Michelle, USA

I emailed my boss, Julie, asking her for annual leave and advised her when I wished to start my maternity leave except my boss never got the email...I had emailed it to

the admin lady, also called Julie, at my boys swimming club! D'oh!
Jenny, UK

I'm losing things a lot, and they always turn up in silly places. I've found my phone in the fridge, my make-up in the cupboard with the pots and pans, and this morning, after about a week of searching, I found my credit card in the box of 'Frosties!' After I'd reported it stolen too. Urgh!
Leanne, UK

When I decide I need to pick something up sometimes I will randomly drop the thing in my other hand. This includes drinks and food!
Louisa, USA

Shortly after having my first Son I was leaving a busy grocery store, after packing the groceries away and putting my Son safely in his car seat I was headed to sit in the driver's seat. I walked behind my car to get around it to get in but for some unknown reason I opened the back door and sat in and shut the door. I didn't even realise what I had done for a good minute or so as I was just sitting there looking out the window! Ha Ha! Then I had to get back out of the car and hop in the driver's seat. There had to be people watching!
Helen, USA

I forget my size all the time, I parked in a space next to a post the other day and then couldn't squeeze my bump

out so I had to climb across to the passenger side and get out!
Sarah, UK

One day I went into the toilets at the Bingo place and couldn't for the life of me figure out where the exit was! I had to literally wait for someone else to wash and dry their hands so I could follow them out! I confuse myself sometimes.
Emma, UK

I was thirty nine weeks pregnant and decided I would drive to the shop (despite being way too big to fit behind the wheel). Well I grabbed the keys off the table, locked up and headed outside to the car but the car wouldn't unlock no matter how often I pressed the unlock button. What wound me up was I could hear it unlock but the door wouldn't open.
Cue a horrendous pregnancy tantrum, crying my eyes out and swearing at the car. Well my Partner's Parents live two doors up, heard the noise and they came to see if I was okay. By this point I was sat slumped on the floor literally crying my eyes out.
How did I hear the car unlocking without the doors opening you ask? I had my Boyfriend's van keys in my hand, which was right behind me and it was the van's locks I heard opening all the time! They've never let me live it down.
Linda, UK

I was opening the fridge door repeatedly wondering why it had started playing a tune when I did so. Then I realized it was my mobile phone in my fleece pocket!
Charlotte, UK

I was in town and had been shopping. I was in tears because someone had stolen my car. I looked in purse to find money to make a phone call (oh the days before mobiles!) and found my return bus ticket. I had come on the bus!
Lucy, UK

I burst out crying last week while loading the shopping onto the conveyor belt because I couldn't reach into the trolley to get the last few bits because of my bump! The young lad serving me didn't know what had happened Ha Ha!
Lauren, UK

My memory was seriously bad towards the end of my pregnancy. My poor Husband had to remind me of everything, including my name, age etc! When asked I would go blank and say I don't know. Then take five minutes to remember!
Victoria, UK

Me and my Husband were walking down the street:-
Me: "Where are we going?" *mindlessly follows*
Husband: "Argos." (As we were passing Greggs Bakery)
Me: "Why? Ooh Greggs!"

Husband: "Because you wanted to go two minutes ago.
Do you still want to go?"
Me: "No I want a cake. I hate Argos!"
Oh the hormones!
Kelly, UK

Pregnancy brain is the worst so far this pregnancy, I'm always forgetting things. I tried paying for my food shopping with a receipt and just stood there looking at the Woman serving like, why are you still looking at me? Cue my Husband laughing his head off and telling me what I had done, then when I finally paid her I forgot to take my shopping!
Then there was the problem of making my Husband his coffee in the mornings, I would make it then either put it in the cupboard or the fridge and take him a bottle of milk or jar of coffee!
Toni, UK

I actually got ready for work one morning, and as I walked out into the garage I thought to myself, "Wow, it's really cold out today" so, I bent over to put my shoes on and saw that I had forgotten to put my pants on! Good job I noticed before I went out!
Alex, UK

My Mom was pregnant with twins, when I was thirteen years old. We went to the grocery store one day, she had on a dress, and her big girl panties fell to the floor and she just stepped out of them and kept going, like nothing had

happened! Kodak Moment for sure!
Isla, USA

I came home from work all tuckered out, and I looked into my crab aquarium. Now the entire time I have had this one crab I haven't liked it. It's boring. It never does anything but sit in its shell. So I am home from work, look up into the aquarium and burst into tears. My crab had apparently died. My Husband was like, "Honey, what's wrong?" All I could say was, "You let my crab die!" My hubby just laughed at me.
Diane, USA

About a month or so ago, around when I finally got my appetite back, it was nearing dinner time. In a restaurant I walked by one of the serving lines, and the server asked me if I knew what I was having. I said something like, "oh probably the chicken, and I might have some pasta too." But she was actually referring to the baby, as in was I having a boy or a girl. I had to laugh at myself, but you could tell where my mind was at!
Carly, USA

They say pregnant women are supposed to be more absent-minded than usual.
I didn't really notice much of a difference between now and my pre-pregnancy absent-mindedness, until the other day.
I was making oatmeal for breakfast, since it was quick, easy, and filling. I opened the package, dumped the contents into the trash can, and stuck the package in my

bowl before I had realized what had happened.
Now my Husband makes my breakfast!
Terri, USA

I was with my Husband, getting a comprehensive anomaly scan when I was starting my sixth month of pregnancy. I guess they check for the development of all the baby's organs etc. The Moment I saw my baby on the monitor, I started blabbering, making incoherent and stupid observations about the baby. The Doctor was pointing out the various body parts of the baby and when she came to the hands, I blurted out" Oh my God! The hands are already there!" Now I know how stupid this sounds! The Doctor said "What do you mean? Already there? They have always been there!"
The baby had one of its hands on its forehead and my Doctor was joking saying "the baby seems to be saying "Oh my God! My Mommy doesn't know anything about me." We had a hearty laugh - me, my Husband and the Doctor. I will definitely share this incident with my baby when he or she will be able to appreciate it!
Nicky, USA

Well, so far I thought (six weeks into my pregnancy) everything was going pretty uneventfully. I love to cook, and so I was making my Husband fajitas and Mexican rice for dinner, and while doing so, straightening up the kitchen. Well, as I'm putting the last seasonings on my homemade sauce and everything else, I noticed it didn't taste very 'Mexican-y' so I started shaking on more and more chili powder. I looked down in shock to see that I've been dumping Paprika on everything! I burst into tears...

hysterically, snot and all. I flopped myself on the kitchen floor, as my Husband runs in. As I'm sobbing I noticed the floor is wet, and I realize that I must have put the wrong detergent in the dishwasher, and it was foaming out of the sides, and there were bubbles and water everywhere. My poor Husband is trying to console me, and I just started laughing and crying at the same time, and couldn't stop. At this point he just says while trying his best not to laugh, "I love you, I like paprika, and look, now you don't need to mop!"

Rachel, UK

After researching online what I can do to not be so pale, I came to the understanding that there's not much I can do, so I went to the mall to look at dresses for the summertime. I hated everything so when I got home I was lying in bed watching TV, eating Animal Crackers. When my Boyfriend came home he asked how my day went I started bawling, telling him I was fat and pale and I was going to be stuck that way all summer long and there was nothing anyone could do about it. This being the first time I freaked out, he just looked at me and didn't really know what to say except repeating "you're not fat, you're pregnant" over and over again. I yelled very loudly that "it doesn't matter if you're pregnant it still makes you look fat!"

Nicki, USA

I seem to be forgetting everything! I was on the phone with my Mom after leaving my Dad's house, and I got all the way to the end of the street before I realized I was on

the house phone!
Missy, USA

I drive an SUV and my boyfriend drives a truck so we have a cheap little car that we drive to places that are far away. Well I drove it to my Parents' house and then didn't feel good so he came and picked me up and we left the cheap car there. The next night we decided to go and pick it up. Well I went inside *my* car which was at *his* house and grabbed my phone, and got into his truck. We were halfway to my Parents' house and he asked if I had the keys to the cheap car (which I had put on *my* set of keys). After driving for forty minutes we got to my house and I couldn't find my keys, they weren't there. I ran into my house to at least tell my Parents that we weren't staying and I looked through my purse again, and at some point took out my wallet. Well the whole way home he complained about how he told me to make sure I had my keys, blah, blah, blah. Well when we got back to the house I tried opening my car door, I had locked my keys in my car and the spare set was in my car as well. So the next day I called a locksmith. When they came I Realized I had forgot my wallet – it was at my Parents' house. After finally getting my keys my boyfriend made me drive to my Parents' house in my car to pick up the cheap car. What a day!
Andrea, USA

I am only nine weeks pregnant but judging by the growth of my boobs you'd think I was almost full term. I started at about a 32B and am now a 36B. Anyway, the other day I was at a friend's Opera wearing a low cut shirt to show

off my new décolletage. I'm walking through the hallway after just scarfing down dinner when I notice that every eye is upon me. Thinking, "Yeah, that's right. I'm a hot sexy pregnant Woman. Feast your eyes." I start strutting along like I am something else. I turn and walk into the bathroom feeling supremely confident. I use the toilet, walk out to wash my hands and check my makeup and notice that a large piece of green pepper is stuck right in the cleavage. Hot and spicy indeed!
Jill, USA

This afternoon I was looking for diaper bags online. I didn't even know that I was doing it, but apparently I was sitting there cooing, "Do we like that one? Mommy loves that one!" My Husband came in the room with a weird look on his face so I said, "What's wrong?" and he said, "Um, babe, are you talking to me? Because I'm upstairs and I can't hear what you're saying but I can tell you're talking." I got all defensive and said, "You're hearing things! I'm not talking, I'm just trying to pick out a diaper bag." So he left and a few minutes later I caught myself squealing, "Ooh look at that one with the brown and blue together!" So I had to go upstairs and apologize to my Husband for getting defensive, but I hadn't even noticed I was talking to the baby!
Katie, USA

I started crying when I saw my first stretch marks and then started crying about everything else, "I want/need to get my hair dyed! I need to work out more! I want a Big Mac! I miss my Dad! I can't find my socks! My glasses are foggy!"

I know, I was being a little melodramatic, but I started giggling soon after and asked my Fiancé, "Are these stretch marks obvious?"
Shannon, USA

I went to the bathroom recently, stood up, pulled my pants up and then reached for the zipper on my jeans. I was going nuts because I couldn't find the darn thing. I literally was lifting my belly to reach underneath only to realize that I was wearing full panel maternity jeans! I felt like an idiot, but had a good laugh telling my Husband about it later, at least no one saw me!
Jenny, USA

A few weeks before I was pregnant I went out and bought a cute springy top for church. When I tried it on it fit perfectly, the wrap was covering up my boobs and everything and I thought I looked good. Well when I had to go to my Cousin's first communion I decided to wear it (although by then I was pregnant and didn't notice I had put on a little extra weight in the chest department. I was at my Mom's house and put it on and I screamed. Everyone in my house came running to the bathroom and I turned to my mom and said "These are not my boobs!" They were nearly popping out of the top! Needless to say we laugh about it now and my Fiancé says that they *are* mine, they are just my 'baby boobies!'
Nicole, USA

Yesterday I went to the bathroom for the umpteenth time and when I went to leave I flipped the light switch

thinking it would flush the toilet and I flicked it a few times off and on before I realized what I was doing and actually flushed the toilet! Yay for preggo brain!
Ashley, UK

I got in my car to leave, just to get out of the house, and never made it because I started bawling. It was just hormones, I had no idea why I was crying. Anyway a Man saw me, and obviously felt sorry for me and gave me a free pizza! A pity pizza!
Kait, USA

Every white shirt I own right now has at least one dribble stain on it from dropping whatever I am eating or drinking on my belly (without noticing). I was cooking the other day and realized (much, much later, of course) I was covering the bottom of my belly in sauce and spreading it around with my bump!
Tyra, USA

Once when I was only a few months pregnant with my first child I was riding in the car with my Parents and little Brother, and I got out of the car and some Lady said "Ma'am there's something stuck to your butt Ma'am." It was an ice cream wrapper, and all my family heard and cracked up, pointing at it. Now even three years later my little Brother still picks on me.
Amira, USA

I was only four months pregnant, but the need to pee happened all the time. I was at a work Christmas party with my Hubby and I told him I needed to go. I proceeded to the bathroom, walked in, went to the stall and started to unzip when the thought occurred to me "Did I just see a urinal on the wall?" I froze. "Am I in the Men's bathroom?" I thought. Right then someone walked in and yes, it was a Man. I could hear him clear his throat, and use the urinal. I totally had a cold and I was holding a hand over my mouth so as not to cough. When he walked out I finally got up the nerve to leave but when I opened the door five people (including the guy who had just been in) were standing there in conversation. My face was so red as walked past them and I mumbled something like "Picked the wrong door" and headed into the Women's. When I finished up and came out they all applauded me! My most embarrassing moment ever!
Carly, USA

The other day I went to the grocery store to grab a few things and got in line at the self-service check out. I was trying to hurry along so that I could pick up my Hubby from work on the way home. So, I had a craving for fresh green beans which I picked up and when I went to ring them up I put them on the scale to weigh them and I knew that I only had like half a pound max but it kept saying six pounds. I was getting so irate and just when I started to mutter profanities I looked down and realized the problem was that because of my height and how close I was standing to the scale, my giant belly was pressing on the scale, making it weigh more! I turned bright red and hoped no one noticed and hurried up and

got the hell outta there! I was so embarrassed!
Molly, USA

I was getting in my car to go somewhere (I don't remember where now) but I got in and put my purse and keys on the passenger seat. I tried putting the car in reverse but I couldn't and I was just sitting there trying to figure out why the car wouldn't move, not realizing that the keys were on the passenger seat and the car wasn't even on! So I felt really stupid and eventually drove off but the next time I got in the car the same thing happened! Thankfully it hasn't happened since but now my Boyfriend won't really let me drive anywhere, can't say I blame him!
Alana, UK

Last week I had just taken my eldest Daughter with me to pick up pizzas for dinner. We were going to have our hands full carrying in two pizzas, sodas and stuff so I turned off the car in my driveway, pointed my car's keyless remote at the front door to my house and got really irritated that the door wasn't opening when I pressed the unlock button. My Daughter just about died laughing, but at the time I couldn't see what was so funny!
Eva, USA

A few weeks ago I went shopping and couldn't for the life of me figure out why my handbag was so much heavier than it was before. Anyway that evening my Husband and I are in the bedroom searching for the remote we looked everywhere and eventually gave up, then bright spark me remembered my handbag was rather heavy and decided just to check (even though I would never do something like that) and there the remote was, in my bag! We had a good laugh at my lost brain cells, but sadly I did the same thing three times after that. I think I get it confused with my mobile and that's why it goes in my bag! At least I know where to look now!   Leila, UK

I work nights and my Boyfriend works days so when I got home one day he hadn't left for work yet and was still lying in bed, so I went to crawl in bed with him and he got up to get dressed for work. I hadn't wanted him to get up and leave me straight away so I started crying and he didn't know what to do, so he asked me to walk him outside so I did (crying still). He turned to hug me and I threw my milkshake on his truck window and ran away! I had no idea I was going to do that, hormones can be pretty funny!
Kayla, USA

I was only about eight weeks along so I wasn't expecting the whole going nuts and crying out of nowhere thing to start so early. Me and my Fiancé went to get some ice cream. Well when we got to the ice cream shop I saw they had hot dogs and I suddenly had to have one. I asked for my usual hot dog with mustard. After waiting ten minutes and repeating our order three times we finally got our food (the girl was new). Normally this wouldn't bug me too much but that day it really did. Well I opened

my hot dog to see that she pretty much put a whole bottle of mustard on it. I lost it and yelled at this poor girl asking her if she would eat this (holding the hot dog to her). Then I just started crying and yelled "I'm pregnant, sorry," and walked away. My Fiancé just looked at me and laughed. He said he wanted to keep me away from people until I returned to normal! Ha Ha!
Tina, USA

One day I had a half sandwich in one hand, and my cell phone in the other. I nearly took a bite out of my phone instead of my sandwich! I realized what I was doing when I had it about two inches from my mouth. Nobody was around to witness it and make fun of me and I haven't told anyone about it (until now).
Kirsten, USA

I am twenty weeks pregnant and am suffering terribly with 'baby brain.' The other day I asked my Boyfriend "What time is it?" He said "Seven" and I said "O'clock?" He just laughed at me and at the time I couldn't figure out what I had said that was funny, it was a totally logical question!
Rebecca, UK

I couldn't fit into any of my pre-pregnancy jeans at all and I didn't have any maternity ones yet. I have one pair that were always too baggy to wear, so I had been wearing them lately, and I started using a hair tie around the button, but even that was getting snug. One day I was on a long drive, and I unbuttoned and unzipped my pants so I

would be more comfortable (they stayed up when I got up so I forgot). When I had arrived and was in the store and pushing my cart, I noticed it was really cool, right where my pants should be. I looked down to find that my pants were hanging off the bottom of my butt! Just as I noticed and went to pull them up an elderly lady near me said "Hey sweetheart if no one is complaining, it isn't a problem, enjoy the breeze!" I was half mortified, and half in stitches laughing! From now on, I always check, that my pants are on!
Jordan, USA

This morning I was running late for work. I got into my car and realized my gas light was on. Now I live like thirty five minutes from work and there is only one hole in the wall gas station for many miles. I get there and there are two trucks with their trailers parked at the pumps so I think to myself "Great! I really am going to be late now!" As I sit there fuming about having to wait for these trucks that are taking up two pumps each to fill their gas, I realize I am starved and haven't eaten breakfast. Knowing that I will be super late if I stop somewhere else to get food, I decide to get food at this gas station. Finally a truck pulls away and I am able to pull up to pump my gas. I get out, start to pump gas, and go in to get something to eat. I pay and get in my car and start to drive off. All of a sudden I hear a bang on the roof of my car. I get out to see what the hell it was and realize what an idiot I was. I had driven away from the pump with the nozzle still in my car! There I was staring at the nozzle in my gas tank with the hose trailing behind...I had ripped it clean off the pump. I look around and see that the gas station is full of people laughing at me. One lady was laughing so hard, she was

doubled over and holding her sides. I quickly replace the nozzle on the pump and go in to tell the owner I just ripped his hose off the pump. So Embarrassed!
Mya, USA

Pregnancy Accidents and Mishaps:-

The pregnancy 'bump' is the most noticeable thing to other people, but sometimes it can just slip your mind that you have one, or how big it is and you can end up in a sticky situation. I've ended up in one or two myself so I know how embarrassing it can be, however, reading other Women's stories I realise it could have been worse! Whether bump related or not, each of these stories is guaranteed to make you smile:-

Every time I sneeze or cough lately I can't help but pee a little at the same time. My Husband has been tormenting me recently saying every time I do anything, in a really patronising voice "Ooh be careful you don't pee!" Then he laughs at me when I do actually pee, oh the joys of pregnancy!
Nina, UK

I've had lots of people in work touching my tummy in the last couple of weeks and I've only just got a bump starting. When one of them did it I said to her "That's actually my tummy you know, it's not the baby's head!" I think that helped her get the point but she also found it quite funny! It is a bit strange how people think its ok just to reach over and grab a feel though, like we've suddenly waved goodbye to normal personal boundaries! Someone else told me a colleague did it to her and she leant over and had a feel of his nether regions to demonstrate how inappropriate she thought it was! I thought this was pretty funny but wouldn't have had the nerve to do that myself!

Laura, UK

I've just spent the past half an hour absolutely sobbing my heart out.

Now I've calmed down a bit I can see the funny side, kind of. I'm thirty weeks pregnant, and for some reason I'm starting to feel a lot heavier and more off balance. Anyway, I've been doing a lot around the house today, and there happened to be an almost empty plastic washing basket on the floor and alongside it some little polystyrene balls that have fallen out of some packaging, so I crouched down to pick them up, and feeling a little off balance, sat myself on the edge of the washing basket to get them. Within a few seconds I'd lost my balance and fell into the basket. I tried to get out and couldn't, so after what seemed like forever, trying to pull myself out and sobbing, I had to tip the basket over and pretty much roll myself out!

If I didn't feel fat before I most definitely do now. I'm sure it would have been hilarious to watch though!

Belinda, UK

I forget I have a bump sometimes and I try and slide past people and obviously shove them out of the way with my big bump! I then have to apologize and feel really stupid. Oh and the other day I tried to get through a door at work before it closed and got wedged in it, highly amusing for the other staff but a bit of an "OMG let the world swallow me up" Moment for me!
Gemma, UK

I remember bending down to hoover under the sofa with the hoover nozzle when carrying my little boy. My hair got stuck and the hoover sucked loads of it out! It already looked really thin because of pregnancy! I cried a lot but was able to laugh with hubby later on about it!
Susan, UK

The other day I couldn't get into my own car in the parking lot. Two cars had parked on either side of my car and I couldn't open my doors enough to get my bump through! I had to call my Husband (who was a ten minute walk away) to come and help me! I was so angry that I wanted to write a note to put on the other cars. Thankfully I didn't as my Husband stopped me (trying not to laugh at me) and was I able to laugh about it later.
Theresa, USA

I have a big soft ottoman for my big L shaped sectional couch. I propped my feet up the other day and drifted off to sleep. When I woke up I had somehow managed to push the ottoman out too far from the couch but got my

butt wedged between the couch and the ottoman. I was so embarrassed because I couldn't get myself unstuck. I had to call my Mother who lives a few blocks away to come help me out because my Husband wasn't going to be home from work for hours. It's a good thing I had my cell phone handy or I could have been stuck there for a while. My Mom laughed until she was crying before helping me up. I can look back and laugh now. At the time it wasn't funny at all.
If anyone else could have seen me I would have been mortified!
Grace, USA

I was on my hands and knees crawling about on the floor to get the remote as I find it hard to walk, but when I was getting up I had one leg spread wide to the left and the other the same only to the right! I looked like a sumo wrestler getting ready to wrestle. Then I had to waddle like that over to the sofa and plump myself down!
I nearly cried but I nearly laughed, in the end I was just happy I was sitting down!
Madeline, UK

At thirty six weeks pregnant I decided to have a bath, candles, chocolate, book, the whole works. It was total bliss, until I decided to try and get out only to realize I was totally stuck, I let the water out, but my body had become a dam, all the water had drained at the front, but the bath was completely full behind me. I spent ten minutes shivering and crying, until I eventually shouted my Husband. He came up, laughed hysterically and asked

why I'd not shouted before. I told him it was because I
didn't want to wake the kids. I felt ridiculous!
Amanda, UK

I remember going into a burger bar with my Mum and
Nan and proudly announcing that I could still just about
squeeze into the seat (you know the awful seat and fixed
tables). Of course that was before I had actually eaten or
drank anything. I was mortified when we finished and I
couldn't get out, especially when my Nan announced it to
the staff and a full café!
Tracy, UK

My story happened when I was about eight months
pregnant with my first. I went into the ladies room at
work, for the millionth time that day. This particular
bathroom only had two stalls. The larger stall was
occupied, so I took the smaller one. When I had finished,
I turned sideways to open the stall door. The door
opened as far as my tummy and wouldn't budge. I ended
up wedged between the wall and the stall door. The
person in the other stall had already left, so I was stuck in
there for about 5 minutes until a customer came in and
helped me get unstuck!
Sam, USA

Well I seriously think this was the funniest thing that has
happened to me so far. I am currently thirty three weeks
pregnant with my first child so every single experience is a
new one for me. Not only new, but absolutely a clueless
experience. When I first felt my child move I thought I

had gas so I was trying to pass gas all night not realizing that what I was actually feeling was what I had been waiting for since the day I found out I was pregnant - my little fluttering baby.

So a few days ago I was driving home in 5 o'clock traffic, and before I left work I had gotten a bottle of Sprite because I was feeling really woozy. With my first drink I felt him bouncing around and he seemed to love the Sprite, so as the traffic started moving I felt this pressure on my belly button that was terrifying. Not painful just awkward. I was so scared to look down because I thought I was going to see an infant's foot crawling out of my body. So as I mustered the courage to look down I saw a clear as day imprint of my Son's foot protruding out of my belly button. I quickly pressed it in so I wouldn't freak myself out any more than I already did!

I vowed after that...that I would never drink Sprite again!

Kim, USA

When I was about seven months pregnant with my first Daughter, I was getting up about three or four times a night to use the bathroom. One night, about three in the morning, I woke up because I had to use the bathroom. In my still-sleepy mind I thought, "I don't need to turn the light on, I can make it there and back without it." That would seal my fate. I walked to the bathroom, sat down and was instantly stuck in the toilet with my rear end in the water - my Husband had neglected to put the toilet seat down and my hugely-pregnant body was now wedged in there. I yelled for my Husband. He got up and came running into the bathroom, flipped on the light and began laughing hysterically! I was livid! He had to help pry me out of the toilet, and has never forgotten to put

the seat down again. (I think he's afraid what would happen to him if I were ever put in that position again!)
Hayley, USA

My Boyfriend and I had gone to see my Sister and her family. Well my Sister just wouldn't give up on my clothes, she really thought it was ridiculous that I was trying to wear my regular jeans (I was about five months pregnant). So she dragged me shopping and stood there giving me this really disapproving look as I shifted through the rack. Finally I broke down and picked out a pair of maternity trousers, hoping to just go to the checkout line and get out of there. No such luck! She dragged me over to the dressing rooms, practically threw me in one, and slammed the door. Not too soon after I realized there was no knob on my side! I was in these stupid pants and locked in the changing room with no escape route. Finally I decided that I was tired of being in there so I slowly crawled under the door, right in front of this lady who was with her little girl. I don't think I've been that embarrassed in a long time! My Sister and Boyfriend couldn't stop laughing, there were actual tears coming out of their eyes!
Alana, USA

I was about eight months pregnant with my first baby and I was at Church. I was wearing a long broomstick skirt and some support pantyhose. I had to go to the bathroom during church (of course) so I went to the bathroom and walked back to my pew. As I reached my pew I slid my hand behind my butt to make sure my skirt would lay down nicely as I sat down. I was horrified to feel a large

bunch of fabric underneath my pantyhose. I jerked the skirt out of my pantyhose and sat down as quickly as I could. I had walked all the way back from the bathroom, and to our pew at the front of the sanctuary with my skirt tucked into the back of my panty hose and I did not know it. To make things worse, when I got my skirt out a piece of toilet paper came out with it. Needless to say I was more than a little embarrassed!
Kerry, USA

When I was about eight months pregnant with my now three year old Daughter I was working at a factory. Not many women worked there. It was during the last break of the day and the break room was filled with people. In the vending machines they had these chips that I had become addicted to so every time that slot was refilled I would buy as many of them as I could. Well about halfway through this 'shopping spree' I dropped a quarter on the floor. I bent over to retrieve it but my hands were full of bags of chips and I lost my balance. Down I went and I couldn't get back up! There I was rolling around on my back surrounded by the chips I just had to have and quarters. I was mortified. To make matters worse the entire room was laughing at me and not offering to help me up. Finally one kind soul came over and I was back on my feet. I quickly gathered up my chips, quarters and as much of my dignity as I could and left.
Cherie, USA

When I was thirty six weeks pregnant I was lying in bed watching a movie. When I had got up I had a lot of leakage coming out so I panicked and said to my Husband

"my water has broken!" So I went to Labor and Delivery and found out that my water had not broken, I had peed myself! How humiliating! My Boyfriend had already called people and told them and then had to break the news to them that my water didn't break I peed myself! I guess my little Man had been putting so much pressure on my bladder I hadn't noticed it when I was sitting down!
Jackie, USA

I'm twelve weeks pregnant and apparently most of my weight is in my butt right now. I dropped my car keys rushing to work and when I bent down to pick them up my scrub pants split right down the back. I and my colleagues couldn't help but crack up for about half an hour!
Shauna, USA

I was out in town, shopping for some maternity clothing as this was my first pregnancy and I had really underestimated how big I was going to get, and nothing fitted me anymore. I had also outgrown all of my shoes so I had my sandals on. Anyway, I was walking along the busy high street and my foot got caught on something. I stopped and tried to pull my foot out of whatever I stood on but it's really stuck. I couldn't see what I'd done because I couldn't see my feet any more. I kept on pulling, crying now and almost hysterical, loads of people staring at me, when some kind lady came over and told me "It's okay" and she undid my shoe, removed it from what it was caught on (I was so relieved that I forgot to ask what it was) and put it back on again for me! I could hardly even look at her, I was so embarrassed, but I

thanked her and went on my way. After that I never went shopping on my own again! I never told my Husband what happened as I would never live it down!
Eve, UK

When I was about eight months pregnant, Hubby and I were crossing the street to go to our friend's baby shower. Well, trying to hurry across as cars were coming, I stumbled. No big deal, I'm clumsy so I'm used to the occasional stumbling, but this time with all the extra weight in front I could not for the life of me get my balance back! I just 'wind-milled' with my arms all the way across the street until finally I made it to the other side, gave up and just fell on my hands and knees. I was okay except for a few scrapes. I can't imagine what the oncoming cars were thinking watching me going down the road!
Charlotte, USA

I had just got a glass of water and it was filled all the way up, I sat down and set the cup on my belly not expecting anything to happen. Well I'm watching TV and the baby starts to kick. I didn't think anything of it because he wasn't kicking very hard, so I focused my attention back on the TV. Next thing you know my water spills all over me! He kicked me so hard that he spilled my water, now I know not to put anything that can be spilled on my belly. Ha Ha!
Jennifer, USA

The other day our poor dog puked on the rug, well I took one look and then I threw up as well. My Husband went to clean up the dog puke and mine, but then he threw up, so of course that made me throw up again, needless to say I was the winner of the vomit Olympics at our house. The whole time I was laughing as I puked, it was all just too much!
Bryony, USA

I got in the bath tub last week, because I was so sick of taking showers. I found out I couldn't shave while in there so I called my fiancé to come and shave my legs. He thought it was so funny. Well to make it worse, after he left I was trying to get out of the bathtub and couldn't. I had already let all the water out, and I was freezing sitting there. So an hour later, after he comes home from Wal-Mart, he finds me in the bathtub crying. He thought that was the funniest thing he had ever seen. Now he stays around, and I refuse to take baths, only showers!
Martine, USA

During my last pregnancy I had horrible gas and it smelled awful. It was around lunchtime at work and I was in the break room. No one was in there at the time so I let one go. Shortly after someone came in so I played dumb and said "Eww do you smell that?" Like the smell was there before I got there. My co-worker thought it smelled like a gas leak and I guess they've had the problem before so he actually called the Fire Department and cleared the entire building! I kept my mouth shut and to this day my Husband and I laugh about how my farts can clear an

entire building!
Ana, USA

I was twenty seven weeks pregnant and I was wearing a white t-shirt. I walked into the elevator at work where there is a full mirror and realized you can tell that my nipples are hard, plus my belly button sticks out! It's quite a funny thing to see. I had to put a jacket over me because I knew people must be looking! Ha Ha! It looked like two eyes and a nose!
Rebecca, USA

I was ten weeks pregnant and had just bought a beach chair from K-Mart. I didn't feel like waiting for my Mom to go into one of the stores and wanted to sit in the chair instead. Well I sat my huge self down and fell right on the ground with the chair with my feet in the air screaming "Help!" My Mom came running to my rescue (while laughing) which I did not find funny. I was annoyed because a guy was in a car directly in front of me on a cell phone and laughed at me before asking if I was okay. The thing is I may have only been ten weeks but I was visibly pregnant, maybe even looked like I was four months and no one helped me. They just laughed!
Amy, USA

When I was pregnant with my first Daughter, I was to be induced on a Monday. Well, the Friday before I was only working half a day, that way I could go and finish up some last minute errands and have the entire weekend to get everything finished at home. Right before I got ready to

go, I went to the bathroom. I came out and started getting my purse and things together when all of a sudden Woosh! My pants were wet! I thought *Holy Cow, my water broke!!* Well, my hubby was at work 40 miles away and I couldn't find anyone else to help me. I also forgot to mention I worked at the Sheriff's Dept at the time. So my boss, the Sheriff, had to drive me to the hospital in his patrol car! Lights and sirens all the way! I finally got hold of my hubby and he met me at the hospital about thirty minutes after I got there. Well, guess what? After they did the exam and used that litmus paper to see if it was amniotic fluid, it turned out I had just peed myself! I was like "I just went before it happened!" Apparently my Daughter had decided to drop and engage into my pelvis even more and had squashed my bladder, making what pee was left in there rush out. I was so embarrassed! But, needless to say I went into labor that night anyway after I got back home and she was born the next evening. I never told a soul what actually happened!
Donna, USA

I was in the bedroom the other night while my hubby was in the bathroom. I was already all set for bed, I had my PJ's on and everything, I was just looking in my wardrobe for a shirt I wanted to wear to work the next day. Out of nowhere I sneezed and I swear I didn't just tinkle a little bit, I peed all over the floor and then I started crying. My hubby came into the room and I was standing there with no bottoms on and just my shirt crying, saying I had to take a shower and to just get me the mop. He was laughing and trying to go see how much I peed and I kept

pushing him away. It was the most embarrassing thing ever!
Ellie, USA

I was fourteen weeks pregnant and my clothes were not really fitting anymore but I just refused to buy maternity clothes so early! One day I put on my favorite jeans but I just couldn't button them, they fit fine everywhere apart from the belly so I wore them to Walmart. They were on my hips fine the whole time I was in the store but when I got to the register to pay I just felt different and the cashier pointed out that my pants were around my knees! I've since bought some maternity jeans!
Jocelyn, USA

I'm twenty nine weeks pregnant right now and just yesterday I was coming home from work and I was feeling so uncomfortable in my work clothes, I quickly went to change into my shorts and t-shirt. Now that my tummy takes up the greater half of my body, I have to bend my legs higher than I did before when I want to change my pants. Well I guess I was in so much of a rush when I got home that I was moving too fast and sprained a muscle in my butt while I was changing into my shorts! Now, not only do I waddle when I walk, I limp too!
Anna, USA

I am now overdue and about a week ago I decided that while I was walking up the hill to my house, I would do some lunges to see if I could get the baby to come. Well that didn't work, all it did was move the baby right onto

my bladder and I partially peed myself instead! I walked up the rest of the hill with my knees together for fear I would fully pee myself! So attractive!
Brandy, USA

My breasts got very sore last week while I was driving and when I was stopped at a red light I was rubbing them absent mindedly without realizing a police car had pulled up beside me and the two male officers were getting quite a kick out of me massaging my breasts! I was so embarrassed! I had to sit there feeling their eyes on me until the light changed! I didn't look over again, I was too mortified!
Michelle, USA

I was about twenty weeks pregnant and for an early Christmas present my Husband and I bought my Dad a recliner. Well I went to sit in it, not realizing just how hard I fell back into it. The whole thing went backwards and I came about three inches from the sliding glass door but all I could do was start laughing! Then of course since I was laughing so hard I 'marked' my Dad's chair and my Sister, who was also pregnant, 'marked' the loveseat from laughing at me!
Brianne, USA

I am twenty weeks pregnant and the other day I was getting ready for bed and we just recently bought a new bed frame. It's about three and a half feet off the ground so I was just trying to figure out how to get on it and as

my Husband walked in the door I was crawling my way onto it just like a little kid does to get on a couch. He was laughing so hard he had to go and pee! Ha Ha!
Kayla, USA

Let me start off by saying I am a plus size Woman with a pretty big chest so I have a hard time finding a bra that fits correctly. When I was nine months pregnant and needed to go to the store I really dressed up hoping it would make me feel better. I was walking through the store and all eyes were on me. I loved it, it was just the boost I needed that day (or so I thought). When I got out to my car I looked down and noticed that one breast had popped out under my bra so with my tight fitting shirt on it was oh so obvious! So everyone had been looking at my very lop sided breast as I was proudly strutting my stuff!
Louisa, USA

I was only five and a half weeks pregnant and I was sitting at work. I felt like I had to throw up and I thought it would pass because it had done before, so I sat at my desk and for a split second it went away. All of a sudden it came back and I thought "should I take the garbage can with me or not?" I didn't but decided to walk/run to the far away bathroom (when I say far away I mean on the other side of the building). I tried to only take deep breaths in and small breaths out so I wouldn't throw up. I knew that once I breathed out I would spew everywhere. Down the hall I see a Man that I know will be passing me soon, and I prayed that he wouldn't say anything to me but he said "Hello" and me being me I had to be polite and say it back although I knew I would be losing some of the air supply I was storing. I got down the hallway where the bathroom room is and I threw up a little in my hand. I started to lightly jog. I shoved open the bathroom door with my right shoulder and then comes the big burst. I threw up more in my hand and it was spurting out around my face and onto the floor. I knew I had no time to open a stall so I went right to the sink. I heaved up the last of it while thinking the whole time "I wonder if I threw up my pre-natals?"

After I was done washing my hands I look up and see my face covered in grainy specs of cracker bits. I quickly wipe it off and in comes a co-worker. I tell her to be careful where she steps as I frantically grab for the paper towels. She asked why and I said because I threw up all over the floor. I didn't wait for her to gasp because I didn't want to hear it so I went right into telling her "Don't worry, I'm pregnant." She giggled as she saw me wiping off my water drenched face. Oh the joys of pregnancy!

Lisa, USA

I was eight months pregnant and suffering from the most awful gas in the world. I was home with my dog and my neighbor was outside helping me with some yard work. I had to pass this gas and I figured that since he was outside he wouldn't be any the wiser. So, I drop this bomb that comes out so loud that the baby in my tummy jumped, my dog thought that it was someone knocking on the door and started barking, and my neighbor freaked out and poked his head in the door to see if I was okay. There I was with a bright red face, trying to explain that everything was fine until the horrendous odor hit my neighbor! He got a funny look and started to back out of

the door before I could even begin to blame the dog. I have rarely been so embarrassed in my life!
Amy, USA

I was driving and my boyfriend was in the passenger seat. We were at a stoplight and I got the urge to throw up so I opened the door quickly with a bunch of people staring at me and threw up. As the light turns green I continued on. I again got another queasy feeling so I pulled over and just went for it. A cop pulled up behind me (and I was only seven weeks so I wasn't obviously pregnant). He accused me of having been drinking and I tell him that I am pregnant and I just have morning sickness. He told me he's heard that before (I thought it was weird that someone would actually make that up and try to pass it off). I got really offended and so emotional that I told the officer if he wanted we could go to the pharmacy real quick and I could pee on a stick to prove it. As we were talking I got the feeling again and threw up all over his boots and he looked at my boyfriend (who sat there patiently, not wanting to interfere with my fight) and said, "She really is pregnant isn't she?" and he apologized and went about his business (embarrassed and with sticky boots!)
Jennifer, USA

Last week it was extremely cold and I had to go and take Teacher's exam. Because of the cold I dressed extra warm in thermals and sweats, but for whatever particular reason that day I decided to put on a nice pair of black sheer thongs (you know ladies still trying to be cute while pregnant). Anyway after the exam I decided to use the

rest room. I pulled everything down (or so I thought) and remembered thinking to myself "how come I'm not hearing the pee fall in the toilet?" I then realized that I hadn't pulled my thong down and was peeing on it! I started panicking but of course I can't take them off because I have too many clothes on with all my extra layers so I had to stuff my underwear with tissue and wait until I got home to change and shower. It wasn't funny at the time but I had to laugh at myself afterwards!
Emma, USA

My Husband and I got married recently and we are both in our twenties and are quite an active couple. So I was four months pregnant and only showing a little. I figured I could fit into some of the lingerie from our honeymoon. Just as my Husband was about to get home from work I rushed into the bedroom and got naked to put it on (it was a green silk teddy thing) so I pulled it over my head and I got stuck. It was trapping my elbows so I couldn't pull it off and I couldn't push it down because of my boobs. My Husband had to come home to his partially naked hysterical wife screaming and crying "Take it off!"
Sian, UK

When I was about five months I was researching everything that a Mother would experience around that time, but one thing I didn't find out about was balance. When I was around twenty weeks my equilibrium was completely off and I would lose my balance. I would be turning around talking to my Fiancé and as soon as I turned my head to finish walking forward there would be a wall. I have run into doorways, walls, and even a post

once at Walmart. It was so embarrassing, but worth it to get your wonderful baby!
Katrina, USA

One of the first pregnancy symptoms I had was an increase in breast size. I got pregnant towards the end of the summer so the weather was still great and I was refusing to stop wearing my usual summer clothes. One day in particular I was determined to wear a very cute top that tied around my ribcage just under my boobs. Putting it on went Just fine but taking it off however was a different story. I got the shirt halfway up over my boobs and it got stuck, and the shirt was covering my head so I couldn't see. I was also wearing black leggings which cut into my newly developed waist fat. So I had to walk out into the hallway calling out for my Boyfriend to help me, with my arms stuck up in the air and my shirt cutting off the circulation to my boobs and not being able to see (and thus walking into a wall). My Boyfriend helped me out of my shirt, but not before collapsing in fits of laughter!
Marianne, USA

With this pregnancy (I am eleven weeks along now) I have been too sick to really have much of a physical relationship with my Husband, so this week I had climbed into his lap for some hugs before work. After the first hug, I was gazing lovingly at my Husband when he gets a weird look on his face, and reaches towards my face. He then yanked on a hair I didn't know was there, growing out of

my chin. I rushed to the mirror and took a look, and there was this HUGE black, curly hair growing out of the bottom of my chin! I quickly got rid of it, but turned bright red, and was so embarrassed. All I kept muttering was "That has never happened before!" While my Husband laughed at me. He reassured me he loves me and that I'm beautiful, but I have never been so embarrassed and felt so ugly!
Nicky, USA

When I was twenty two weeks pregnant I already felt huge and I was over at the In-laws for dinner. While I was there, someone asked where the BBQ sauce was. I was standing by the back door (with the screen on the door), saw the BBQ sauce by the BBQ and went to get it but just plowed through the screen door, even making it two steps outside before I stopped! I took it off the tracks and even bent the frame. I was laughing so hard and everyone else was freaking out checking I was okay. Needless to say, I felt like a huge whale that just destroyed their screen door with ease!
Shauna, USA

When I was pregnant with my Daughter (maybe twelve weeks or so, not showing then) I was getting ready for work one morning, running late as always, and I put on my favorite super low-rise jeans. They didn't have a button, just a two inch zipper. After I got dressed, I bent down to put on my shoes and felt a pop. The zipper had ripped wide open, and the pull was stuck at the top! I had to rip the zipper open and rush to find pants that fit. I called my boss to explain that I was running fifteen

minutes late because I got trapped in my pants! He thought it was hilarious, and I realized that I might need to invest in some stretchy pants!
Melanie, USA

Midwives and Doctor's Appointments:-

The essential part of any pregnancy, your appointments may be routine but they don't always go to plan, sometimes completely the opposite! I've had a few 'interesting' appointments while I was pregnant, it seems a lot of other people have too:-

My friend (who by her skin colour is very obviously of a mixed race background) got told by her Midwife at an appointment that in fact she was not of ethnic origin because it didn't say so on her file and therefore it wasn't true!
Joanne, UK

I went to the antenatal clinic at the hospital and was greeted by the receptionist with "Hello... are you pregnant?"
I looked at her, looked at my huge bump and looked back at her again. No further discussion was needed.
Chloe, UK

During one of my early scans, the sonographer said "I must say, you have lovely ovaries."
What do you say to that? "Thanks, I work out?"
Angela, USA

When I had an internal scan due to my dates being wrong, and them not being able to find the baby on the abdominal scan:
Gynaecologist: "You did get pregnant naturally, right?"
Me: "Yeah."
Gynaecologist: "Good, good. Your ovaries must be in here somewhere then!"
I thought she was bonkers!
Jennifer, UK

My consultant asked the weight of my first Daughter. I told him she was 6lb 6 six weeks early. He went quiet and then said "OMG I bet you're glad you didn't cook her full term, that would have hurt!"
Shirley, UK

After seeing the potty shot after my twenty week scan my Doctor said "Well, definitely a boy. It will be fun to see if his balls will be as big as they look here. After all, the camera adds ten pounds." I didn't know how to answer that!
Donna, USA

After we had our gender scan at twenty weeks the Doctor told my Husband that our Son either had an erection or a future in adult video. (My Husband still talks about this to everyone!)

Before that, just after the actual scan, he said "Right, now I'm going to check your breasts", so without any warning pulls up my top and starts grabbing and pinching at my boobs and says "You have perfect breasts." At this point my Husband is sitting there with a totally gobsmacked look on his face. So I looked at the Doctor and said "Thanks" and he quickly fills in "For breastfeeding, that is". I thought this was all too funny!

Also my Brother in Law swears babies can fart in the womb even though they can't. We had an hour long discussion about it and he still thinks he's right!

Shelley, USA

I went along for my scan today, and wow the room was busy! Me, Hubby and three others, not quite sure who they all were, but they explained that it was going to be a trans-vaginal scan (half expected it to be but ugh).

Well there I am lying there holding on to dear life trying not to slip! (Why they can't use the other type of chair that you can lie your legs on I don't know!) Luckily I had a gown over my legs to cover my modesty while the three of them tried to get the chair up and back, (not very successfully!)

Out comes that wand, and after poking and prodding me she started looking at the screen! I'm lying there thinking "oh what's she doing? It's not even in!" She must have realised as she had a look down there and fiddled around, I'm lying there thinking "oh God how embarrassing!" But I've got to tell her before she tries to look for the baby

there!   So I say "umm excuse me you're going the wrong
way, that's going to be in my bum in a minute!"
Well everyone had a good chuckle at my expense.
She had another go and then said to me "Umm do you
want to put it in yourself?" I didn't know whether to
laugh or what!
I said "No, not really"!
Faye, UK

When I had my ultrasound at 14 weeks, the Tech was
trying to measure the baby but it was all curled up, so she
started shaking the probe on my tummy to get it to
straighten up and she was shouting "EARTHQUAKE,
AHHHHHH!" It was so funny and I was trying not to laugh.
It surprised the baby and it just moved a little but it still
stayed curled up. I wondered at the time if any other
Techs used this method!
Cathy, UK

I was at the Doctor's office a couple of weeks ago and I
had to have my first physical. I was really nervous because
being pregnant doesn't exactly make you feel like the
most attractive thing in the world, and I feel like I can
never be clean enough. So when the Doctor left and told
me to undress and put on my gown, I immediately went
for the paper towels and the sink. I started with my arm
pits because I knew he was going to check my breasts, so I
start wiping them down with a wet paper towel, and I just
keep on going. My Sister was in the room at the time and
burst out laughing. I completely forgot she was sitting
there. She said "He'll be back in a few minutes. You can't

just take a bath in the Doctor's sink!"
Maxine, USA

While at my last appointment (when I was twelve weeks pregnant) I was getting dressed and putting my bra back on, which was a strapless that hooked in the front. It was my favorite and so comfortable, well I went to latch it in the front and it broke and shot across the room! My boyfriend was laughing hysterically and I was just in shock. I tried to put it back together the best I could just to get out of the office and go home to get a new one so I could go to work. I put my coat on and walked out of the room with my arms crossed fearing that it would fall off from under my coat. I got out safely but as soon as I got in my car it fell off! I was relieved it didn't fall off before that but I couldn't stop laughing! I had always been pretty small in the chest area but had gone up a size since being pregnant so my boyfriend thinks it's funny that my dream finally came true, my boobs broke a bra!
Claire, USA

During my last pregnancy, I was extremely off balance most of the time and I ended up somehow missing the top stair on our staircase and slid the entire way down on my butt. I had to be monitored at the hospital for six hours and had a lovely rug burn on the cheek of my rear. I can't tell you how many Nurses and Doctors had to come in and felt it was necessary to poke at it, as if the whole experience wasn't embarrassing enough!
Josie, USA

I was in the hospital overnight when I was twenty nine weeks because the baby was giving us a scare and I was having contractions. Well, I had to pee every couple of minutes as every pregnant girl does. Every time I peed I had to tell the Nurse so she could check it. Well, I had to pee again and my old pee was still in the pot, so I woke my Husband up and said "what should I do?" He said "they have call buttons babe." So I went into the bathroom and pulled the string in there. I started hearing these alarms going off out in the hallway and at the front desk. As I'm standing there holding my pee four Nurses come running in and my Husband came in behind them, he was grabbing my arm asking what was wrong. I looked at them all and like a little kid I said, "I just have to pee!" the Nurses started cracking up and one pointed to the string I pulled. She said "Hun this an emergency string, if you need anything that isn't an emergency all you have to do is ring the Nurse bell right here." I was so embarrassed! Needless to say I blamed it all on my Husband and they ended up laughing at both of us.
Katie, USA

Me and my Boyfriend went to my first Doctor's appointment and the first thing the Nurse asked when we got into the room was, "So you're pregnant?" My Boyfriend (looking very serious) looked at me and said "You said we were here for birth control!" You should have seen the look on the Nurse's face, she didn't know what to say! Finally we convinced her he was kidding. At the same appointment they go to do my pap and he gets up to leave the room but before walking out the door he turns around, looks at the wand they use and says "careful, I did that and now she's pregnant!" I went bright

red! The nurse replies "no, had you used toys you wouldn't be here!" It was so funny but embarrassing at the same time!
Josie, Nevada, USA

The worst thing that ever happened to me during pregnancy with my Son was when I got to my very first Doctor's appointment at about seven weeks along. I felt queasy (as you do) and couldn't stop myself throwing up all over the waiting room which started a chain of other pregnant Women throwing up after me. I think there were four Women who were sick in about a three minute timespan. It was pretty awful!
Jane, UK

I had scheduled my Doctor's appointment to try to determine the baby's gender. I had myself convinced it was a girl and every time someone would contradict me I would get really heated (I chalk it up to hormones of course). So everyone stopped arguing with me when I called my child a she, well everyone except my Father, that is. He was dead set on a Grandson. Well the big day came and my Dad went with me because my Fiancé was in another state at the time. We got in the room and I settled in for my ultrasound, perfectly ready to gloat when the technician announced I was going to have a girl. Not even twenty seconds into the ultrasound the Tech said "You're having a baby boy, he certainly isn't shy!" My Dad started cheering and clapping like his favorite football team just won a championship and I burst out crying, I mean not just crying but wailing. The Tech got me tissues and tried to comfort me, and all I could say was "I'm

happy, but I've been calling him a girl's name for a month! This is worse than the time I named my male cat Alice! What if he grows up gender confused because of me?" The tech could not for the life of her convince me that the baby really couldn't hear yet. She was almost in tears herself, from laughing at me. Finally the Doctor explained that no, he couldn't hear yet, and then said "But to be on the safe side, stick with strictly boy colors for the first year you dress him okay?"
Terri, USA

Fathers to be:-

They took part in the baby-making but then it's down to the Mother to do the rest, and don't we let them know it! Some try their best to help us, rubbing our feet or holding our hair while we throw up! Others are entirely clueless, but they can be hilarious and that's why they deserve their own section:-

I was in my third trimester and I was having some Braxton Hicks contractions which were making me quite uncomfortable. I had been telling my Husband about them and he was kindly cooking the dinner so I didn't have to do it that night. Anyway, my Husband's Brother called him and he must have asked him how I was feeling. I overheard his side of the conversation, when he said "She keeps getting those 'Braxton Pickles.'"
I tried my best not to let him know I was listening but I was giggling while I composed myself. I still haven't told him he keeps using the wrong name, it cracks me up every time he says it. He does like 'Branston Pickle' so

that must have been where it came from!
Hayley, UK

I wasn't pregnant at the time but I was on the bus into town for some shopping and there were a couple of young guys sat in front of me having a conversation about one of their pregnant Girlfriends. I was stifling my giggles the whole way, it was just too funny! Their conversation went like this:-

1st Guy: "She should have had it by now shouldn't she?"
2nd Guy: "Yeah, she's overdue now."
1st Guy: "So what happens then, you just wait?"
2nd Guy: "Yeah but she said if she goes two weeks past the due date they'll take her into hospital and juice her."
1st Guy: "Juice her?"
2nd Guy: "Yeah, I don't know what happens, maybe they squeeze her, you know? I'm not sure."
1st Guy: "Oh right, I never heard of that before. But I wouldn't know would I? I've got no kids yet."

There were some other ladies who overheard too and they were laughing, I don't think anyone had the heart to say anything to them. The Dad to be had obviously heard that the Mum to be was going to be 'induced' and got confused. The poor Lads seemed genuinely clueless!
Sally, UK

I went into labour with my first baby and Hubby and I went to the hospital but I wasn't far along enough and they sent me home to get some rest. Yeah right! Like that was going to happen!
I did try though and got into bed whilst Hubby was on the sofa downstairs. He promptly fell into a deep sleep and I

managed to get a few winks in too after a while. However I was quickly woken with horrible contractions, so I yelled down to him "It's time to go!" He literally jumped off the sofa and ran full pelt up the stairs. Seeing that I wasn't actually giving birth, he went into the bathroom for a wee. He was stood at the toilet, flies undone, finished his wee and then passed out cold on the bathroom floor with his bits still hanging out!

I was in the throes of a contraction, absolutely peeing myself laughing at the sight of him on the floor and trying to lift him up.

Several hours later, still in labour at the hospital (and feeling very hard done by), I decided to share the story with the Midwives who were howling with laughter as my Hubby just sat there shaking his head, looking like he was going to kill me! Justice was served me thinks!

Amy, UK

When myself and my Partner went to the hospital for my last scan and check-up, we were in a little cubicle waiting for the Nurse. She came in and asked if she could examine me whilst some 'Pupils' watched. I assumed she meant Nursing or Midwifery students so I said "Of course, no problem."

The Nurse arrived five minutes later with about six school kids! They were older ones but still not what I was expecting. I was mortified then when out of the blue my Husband decided to have a joke with them and told them that he wasn't the Father and that he found me outside and decided to bring me in because he felt sorry for me and he didn't even know my name! I didn't know where to look and the poor kids thought he was being serious!

He sees himself as a bit of a comedian, I'm not so sure.
Jane, UK

I fainted in the Dentist's chair when I was seven months
pregnant and they couldn't wake me up! So
embarrassing! The staff still remember it every time I go
in, cringe!
Natalie, UK

When I was about two months away from giving birth I
was in bed eating a bowl of cereal. I started choking on it
and then noticed the bed was wet.
Well, I jumped up, told my other half to phone the
hospital as my waters had gone. He calmly told me that I
had wet the bed. I looked at him in disgust and said "How
very dare you! Our baby is on the way, I don't wet the bed
anymore!" He sighed and agreed to phone the hospital
and I heard him say "Yeah it smells of wee!" Then he put
the phone down, laughing, and told me that the Midwife
asked him to tell me that it was normal for women to wet
themselves during the later stages of pregnancy! Oh the
shame!
Megan, UK

I was a week from my due date with my first Daughter
and having already gone to the hospital three times with
possible pre-term labour, my Fiancé was very anxious and
excited that my due date was finally here. He was so
excited because I was having contractions all day from
walking. He decided to drink an entire half gallon of iced
tea before bed, his intentions being to try to stay up all

night in case I did need to go to the hospital, but he ended up falling asleep around 2.30am.

He woke up around 9.30am and climbed out of bed looking at me lying there sound asleep. He ran into my now Sister-in-laws room and woke her up screaming that my water had broken and it was all over him and the bed and me. She came running and so did everyone else in the house because they were worried about me. I woke up with a room full of people staring at me so I asked "What's going on?" My Fiancé said "Your water broke, are you ok?" Well I replied "No it didn't! Do you think I would be lying here sound asleep if my water broke?" He said "I don't know."

Well I came to find out since that he drank all that iced tea and had peed the bed and blamed it on me! Needless to say he has yet to live that down and now every time we see his family they ask him if he has had any accidents with my current pregnancy. Ha Ha!

Emily, USA

My Husband and I started talking about our finances now that I'm going to be taking pregnancy leave. We were sitting down talking about an estimated amount that we spend on bills and everything and then after putting everything together we came to a conclusion that it won't be that bad.

After our bills were laid out and expenses were discussed, we talked about food and gas and other miscellaneous things. There was a pause and then my Husband turned to me very serious and said "Well, if things get out of control we can ask my uncle to let us borrow his COSTCO card so we can buy the food for the baby" I said, "Well we don't have to worry about that, the baby's not going to

eat that yet!" He said with a blank expression on his face "Well... what *is* the baby going to eat?" Ha Ha!
Aubrey, USA

I was reading about the stages of labor with my Fiancé the other night and when I finally reached the last stage (passing the placenta), my Fiancé asked me "Well what happens the next time we want to have a baby? Don't you like, need your placenta?" I about peed myself! Then explained that you grow another one when you get pregnant again.
Rebecca, USA

I was getting examined by the Midwife and it was the Hubby's first time seeing this. He looked a bit odd and I was just about to ask him if he was okay when he said "Should I close the door?" and winked!
I was so embarrassed at the time, but the Midwife burst out laughing and so did I, then I just didn't know what to do with myself so I kicked him out, the dirty bugger!
Liana, UK

This is our first child and from the moment my Husband found out we were pregnant he's been saying "Honey I can't stand this waiting I want to see my baby now." It has me all smiles every time he says it.
He has been avoiding sex and when I asked why he said "I've never invaded anyone's home before." I nearly died laughing!
Lisa, USA

I remember when I was about seven and a half months pregnant with my Son I had massive cravings for 'Butterfinger Crunch' bars and one day I was standing in the check-out line at Wal-Mart. The cashier was nice and asked if I minded if she asked when I was due. I told her I was due in March. She was a bit plump herself so when she put her hand on her belly and said "I'm due about a month after you" I didn't know what to say. My Fiancé (Husband now) just burst out laughing and said "I thought you were just fat, you really don't look pregnant." I couldn't believe that he would actually tell anyone that, he normally bites his tongue!
Bree, USA

Now that I am pregnant my friends have declared me the designated driver for the next nine months. I'm six weeks pregnant and not really showing yet. We went out to eat together last weekend and everyone ordered their food and drinks. When the waiter got to me I ordered, I don't know if it was the extra jalapenos I ordered, or the amount of food, but the waiter looked at me for a minute and said "I bet my tip you are the pregnant designated driver."
To get back at him when he brought my food my Husband kind of jumped at him and said "Watch your fingers Man! When she is hungry she bites!" The waiter freaked out and jumped back! We laughed for the whole meal! Ha Ha!
Kate, USA

I overheard my Husband talking to toilet. He said "my Wife used to sit on me, now she only sits on you." Ha Ha! He did know I was in earshot though, think it was a hint!
Charlotte, UK

I am thirty five weeks along, and you can definitely feel the baby from the outside kicking full force now, so my Boyfriend is always wanting to feel the baby. Anyway I told him that the baby monitor that I sent for had just come and how I was excited about it. Well he got really excited about it and I wasn't sure why he was so over the top about it. So a minute later he asks if we can take it out of the box and hook it up. Being confused I asked what we were hooking it up to. So he blurts out "Your belly!" Well I didn't get it so I said "What do you mean?" It turns out that he thought the monitor was for hooking up to my belly to see the baby inside! He got so excited only to be crushed! But I couldn't help but laugh. It was so cute but Man, what a dork!
Julia, USA

Last night me and my Husband went to the county fair with his family and some friends. One friend has a one year old Son so my Husband decided to carry him around a little bit to get him used to handling a baby. He looked over at me while this cute little baby is sleeping on him and says, "Honey I'm so ready for this, I just can't wait" and at that exact moment my Husband's face went from a smile to a look of horror. The baby had peed all over my Husband and he lifted him up to find this huge pee spot on his shirt. Then he was holding the baby away from him and running around trying to find the baby's Mom.

Needless to say my Mother-in-Law and I couldn't stop laughing! What was really funny was the fact he had to walk around with pee on his shirt for the rest of the day!
Katrina, USA

Earlier today I had the hiccups, and one way to get rid of them that usually works for me is to hold my breath. So I was holding it, and my boyfriend looked at me and said (in all seriousness) "What are you trying to do? Suffocate the baby?" I kind of looked at him and giggled thinking he was joking and he replied with "No, I'm serious, don't they breathe whatever you breathe, and that's why you can't smoke?" I stared at him until I realize he was indeed serious. I said "Honey, they are not actually breathing air in there, they are breathing in and swallowing amniotic fluid. We can't smoke because the toxins get into the bloodstream to the baby." He just stared at the ground and said "Oh." I really hope the baby gets my genes!
Shirley, UK

On the way to my first Doctor's appointment when I was six weeks pregnant my Boyfriend had his radio turned up pretty loud when all of a sudden he slapped the off button, looked at me and said, "I'm so sorry. I wasn't thinking!" I must have had this weird look on my face because he then explained to me that he read somewhere that loud noises can give a baby the twitches! After wiping my eyes from laughing so hard I finally convinced him that the baby couldn't even hear anything right now. I can't wait to see what else he reads!
Gillian, UK

When I went into labor with my first Son it was about 9:00am and I thought I was just having Braxton Hicks contractions and not real ones so I got up to use the restroom because it felt like I really had to pee. I ended up having a really painful contraction and I fell of the toilet. Every time I thought a contraction was over I would scoot closer to the bedroom to wake my Husband up while yelling for him the whole time (my Husband could sleep through a hurricane). I finally got to the bed and I shook him until he was awake and told him "We need to go to the hospital now!" He turned his head and looked at me and said "Who's in the hospital?" I finally got him up by telling him that if he didn't get up *he* would be in the hospital! I was two weeks overdue and was not waiting any longer!
Rachel, USA

The other day I was watching "A Baby Story" on TV while my Boyfriend slept next to me (he works the night shift so he sleeps during the day). I was watching the birth of a baby and the moment that the baby cried my Boyfriend sat up and looked in the direction of the baby bed that we had set up. He looked for the baby and then looked at me, because I was laughing, and then he laid back down and sighed. It was so sweet, I told him that the baby wasn't here yet so he could relax, and he went right back to sleep! He's going to be a good Daddy.
Maria, USA

I am twenty three weeks pregnant and this happened yesterday. I was putting on a pair of jeans that I knew didn't fit but I was going to try anyway. When my Husband walked into the room and asked why I was lying on the bed struggling to get them on, the button flew off and hit him square in the eye! He still has a black eye and now loves to call me his favorite button popper! That will teach him to question the strange antics of a pregnant Woman!

Jenny, UK

My Husband likes to put his head in my lap when we're watching TV at night. The last two times he laid his head down, he cuddled up close to my belly. Well, my little boy doesn't like having his space invaded. So he punched Daddy in the ear! I laughed and so did my Husband. Then our little sweetie hit him again! I was laughing pretty hard and my Husband told the baby "You stop it!" which prompted another punch! "That's it you're grounded when you come out!" Well, the baby doesn't care and hit him again!

Tori, UK

I was at my Ante Natal class with my Husband, sitting there having a conversation about matters after the birth of our babies as it was the last class. The instructor started talking about the personal decision of whether or not to have your child circumcised. My Husband turned to look at me, dead serious and said "Why haven't we discussed this yet, we discuss everything else, isn't this important?" I looked at him with an amazed expression and said "Honey, we are having a girl!" I still make fun of him about this.

Gina, USA

Pregnancy and young children:-

Why do kids have to be so honest?
The way our little ones grasp the idea of pregnancy can be hilarious, they seem to understand the idea of a baby being inside your belly, but not how it got there or how it comes out (although they will tell you how they think it happens). Some of the funniest stories I've read so far have been about what Children have said or done around us pregnant ladies:-

When I had my 4D scan the other day I was lying there happily watching my boy and my Daughter turned to me and said, "Look Mummy, he's going to be fat like you!" Charming!
Leah, UK

We found out we were having a boy. My Son said to me, "but Mommy I wanted a Sister!" So I said "Well we can't decide what baby is, the baby decides if it wants to be a girl or boy, and this baby wanted to be a boy". He then said "Okay Mommy, but we need to make another baby

in your tummy and I'll tell it to be a girl baby, because I want a Sister."
Lori, USA

I am a teacher and got a surprise last week when speaking to one of the little boys:-
Little Boy: "Is there a baby in your tummy?" *puts his ear to my tummy*
Me: "Erm, maybe, check my bump next week if it is bigger there may be a baby in there."
Little Boy: "Your bump isn't that big."
Me: "Maybe the baby is still small."
Little Boy: "Babies grow in bumps right?"
Me: "Right"
Little Boy: "Do you have two growing up here?" *grabs my boobs*
Me: "No, babies don't grow in there and you can't really touch other people there."
This child is aged five and it was all totally innocent! I nearly fell over laughing.
Maddie, UK

My little boy is always coming out with random funny things! Here's a few:-
I'd just had my scan for my Daughter so was showing him the pictures and telling him about the baby:-
Me: "look, this is the baby in Mummy's tummy, you're going to be a big Brother" *shows him scan picture*
My Son: "How did that get in there? Did you eat it?"
Me and my Husband just burst out laughing and couldn't stop laughing for ages after that!
Also, I was at my friend's house the other day and her

little boy, who is three was messing around and I said "You can't jump about on the sofa, there's a baby in my tummy and you might knock it." He lifted up my top to have a look (and a stroke!) and said "There's a baby in there? How do you get it out?" I called his Mum to explain that one!
Ella, UK

A six year old girl I babysit for was watching my tummy for a while and then looked at me and tactfully said "You look like you're going to have a baby!"
I'm very glad I actually am or I would have been mortified! She then went on to casually say "I think you'll scream when they take your skin off because they have to you know, to get the baby out. Then they put it back on again. You might die."
I kind of went "Erm, no I think I'll be fine. Talk to your Mother about having babies tomorrow!"
It was so awkward, because I hadn't told her about the baby before this, I was waiting for her Mum to approach it with her!
Karla, UK

My eight year old Niece said to my five year old Nephew when she found out I was pregnant "You have to be very careful to not jump on Auntie's stomach as she is pregnant and you might rupture her womb." I couldn't stop laughing. She has had a very broad vocabulary since she was two!
Lauren, UK

I asked my four year old Niece the other day if she thought the baby would be a boy or a girl, and she said "A girl, because *you're* a girl!" Then looked at me as if this was the most obvious thing in the world, and I was a bit stupid Ha Ha!
Tracey, UK

My Nephews think the baby is in my belly button because it pokes out. They always talk into it and when I ask them why they say "So baby can hear us."
I said "No, baby is not in the belly button."
Sally, UK

Today I was asked by my three year old Cousin "When the baby comes out, can I dress it for you?" which I thought was adorable. Meanwhile my other two little Cousins (seven and six) were putting their hands on my bump and asking "When will the baby kick?" and "Is it sleeping?" and all of a sudden the seven year old says to the six year old "The baby is hiding because you're really loud! You've got to talk like this, (whispers) "Hi little baby, it's your Cousin, I love you!" It was so cute!
Cheryl, UK

My three year old Cousin always asks me where the baby is and why I left her at home! I try to explain that she is still in my tummy but he doesn't seem to get it!
Caroline, UK

My five year old Brother asked me if the baby in my tummy would grow into pineapples! I Don't know where he got that from but I did have to laugh!
Julie, UK

My kids have said some sweet and funny things to me since finding out we're going to have another baby. They are 7, 6, and 4.
6 year old: "Mommy, will they have to cut you open to get the baby out?"
Me: "No honey, probably not."
6 year old: "Will they tell you to push?"
Me: (with a smirk on my face) "Yes honey, they will."
6 year old: "Oh! (Spreads her legs) The baby will come out here (points to vagina), right?"
Me: (on the verge of giggles) "Yes honey, that's right."
4 year old: "Mommy does the baby like pop? Gum? Chicken? Potatoes? Salad?" (It goes on... Anything I put in my mouth, I am questioned as to whether or not the baby likes it). These questions are because the kids wanted McDonalds one time and I said that the baby doesn't like McDonalds (it has made me sick ever since I've been pregnant).
7 year old: "Mommy, I know a lot about babies. Did you know the umbilical cord is attached to you?"
Me: "Yes I knew that buddy. Do you know what it's for?"
7 year old: "It feeds the baby cos it can't eat real food yet, right?"
Me: "Yeah, kinda!"
The funniest thing ever was when my kids had a chance to watch a couple of my Mom's cat's kittens being born, and then the seven year old asked me the next day if the baby

will come out of my butt, like the cat!
Helen, USA

My Daughter recently found out I am pregnant with another baby. She later that morning asked me if the baby would be coming out of my tummy (she knows I had a c section with her) or my "big fat bum." Charming!
Chelsea, UK

My four year old Niece said the funniest, cutest thing when I saw her this weekend. Her Mum told her that there was a baby growing in my tummy. Then, when she spoke to my Sister on the phone later she said "Auntie Helen's got a fat tummy, but it's okay because there's a baby growing in it. I'm going to be Cousined!" Then every time anyone spoke too loudly she'd say "Shush, you'll scare the baby." It was so sweet!
Tina, UK

My Son lay down across my lap, facing my belly the other day. He started patting it and said "I love dat baby. I'm gonna look after dat baby." Melt!
Georgina, UK

My Son insists on reading my bump a bed-time story, which I think is very cute. Then he gives it a kiss goodnight and a rub, then gives me a hug and a kiss and tells me "Everything will be fine."
Janine, UK

I had a private scan at sixteen weeks with my Daughter and had a little DVD of her squiggling around. When I showed my Nephew (who is three) I said "Oh look, there is the head, the arms and the legs."
He pointed at the screen and said "And its tail!"
I had to look twice!
Tara, UK

I was at my Sister's the other day and My Nephew was there. The conversation between us went like this:-
Nephew to my Sister: "Are you having another baby Mummy because your tummy is super fat."
Nephew to me: "Shall we play Doctors and Nurses? You be Nurse."
Me: "Ok Doctor, who is here today and what's the problem?"
Nephew: "My Mummy is having a baby and needs to get it out, can you pass me a knife please so I can cut it out?"
My Sister: "OMG you're not delivering my baby like that!"
Stacey, UK

We didn't know how to tell our five year old Niece that we were expecting a baby. We didn't want her to ask where children came from or how it happened, so we sat her down and told her that we were going to have another baby. She looked at me and then at my Husband, and said "Another one?" We both nodded and then she looked at me and said "It was from him biting you huh?" I just cracked up. Funniest thing I have heard in a while!
Shannon, USA

With my last pregnancy my Mom asked my three year old Son if he wanted a baby Brother or a baby Sister.
His reply was: "I want a train!" Ha Ha!
Wendy, USA

I told my little boy that I was going to have another baby and it took him a while to grasp it, then I said "I'm going to get big and fat like this (put my arms out in front of me to show a bump).
He got teary eyed and said "Oh no you can't, you will pop!"
Becky, UK

My friend's conversation with her three year old today:-
Her: "The baby's kicking."
Him: (laughing) "He's kidding? That's kinda funny!"
Her: "No, not kidding, kicking."
Him: (with a very serious look on his face, gets super close to my tummy and says) "Hey! We is not allowed to kick Mama! You goin' be in trouble!"
Joy, USA

When we told the boys I was pregnant and that 'Mumma' had a baby in her tummy the four year old said "Mumma when dat baby come out?"
I said "not for long time, it has to grow first."
He turns to me and said "Are you sure it's not coz baby shy and doesn't want to play with me?"
Kelly, Lakeland, USA

When my Sister was pregnant last year and told my Sons, my eldest who was about three and a half told everyone his Auntie had eaten a baby!, he looked in her mouth then said "Auntie you shouldn't eat babies!"
Bethany, UK

When we found out I was pregnant again my oldest boy wanted a Sister. I told him I couldn't guarantee it was a girl, it could be another boy. His reply was "If you have another boy can we sell him on ebay, and buy a bike instead?" Ha Ha!
Ruth, UK

This morning, I was crouched over the toilet being sick and a little face pops around the door (my four and a half year old). He said "Mummy, I do love you, even when you are being sick, but can you please try not to sick my baby up?" You've got to love kids for making you stay positive!
Katie, UK

Our Daughter told us that babies come out through the 'magic zip' which appears on your tummy, you zip it open to get the baby out and then it disappears after the baby has come out! If only it were that simple!
Keeley, UK

Conversation with my four year old Nephew last month:-
Him: "Auntie, when you have a cup of tea does it burn Cousin Charlie's head?"

Me: "No spud."
Him: "What about when you have a shower?"
Me: "Nope, he's got lots of protection."
Him: "Oh okay. Well what time is he coming out?"
Me: "August."
Him: "Is that my birthday?"
Me: "No, your birthday is in January."
Him: "Well in August we'll play football. I'll teach him."
Megan, UK

My Brother's Girlfriend's Daughter is three. One day I switched my Doppler on in an attempt to stop her running riot around my Mum's house. She picked up the Doppler speaker and started talking into it thinking the baby would hear her. Funnily enough, the baby didn't respond (much to her disappointment!). Our conversation went like this:-
Her: "Why is your baby ignoring me?"
Me: "It's not quite big enough to speak yet."
Her: "Or maybe it's just sleeping?"
Me: "He or she might be, but I still don't think he or she is old enough to talk!"
Her: "He or she? Well, if it's a boy I'm throwing him in the bin!"
Nicola, UK

The other day my Boyfriend's Son, who is five, was sitting next to me and decided to lift up my top so he could speak to my baby through my belly button. He said "Hello baby, would you like to share my sandwich? It's ham!"
Vicky, Telford, UK

A little boy asked if I was fat at playgroup yesterday. When told him "No, I'm pregnant" he replied "Oh congratulations! You can never tell." I nearly wet myself he was only about six!
Marie, UK

The other day after playgroup it was raining so we were rushing to get to the cafe to use up the half hour before our bus. My little boy said "I've got fast legs, like Daddy, but you have got your slow legs on because the baby's getting bigger, but it's okay, when the baby comes you can have your fast legs back!" Ha Ha!
Lesley, UK

My Son is six, he was trying to look through my belly button the other day and when I asked him what he was doing he said he was looking for the baby!
Jess, UK

Once the kids were feeling bubs kicking when one told me quite seriously that "You have to put the baby in time out because you're not allowed to kick!"
Libby, UK

My friend's little girl said to me the other day "If you spin round and round will your baby get dizzy?" Ha Ha! I laughed but I thought it was quite a good question!
Susie, UK

When we were waiting to find out the sex of the baby, my five year old who really has his heart set on a baby Brother kept saying "If it's a girl you will have to take it back to the hospital and exchange it." Ha Ha!
Luckily, we are having another boy so we won't be exchanging!
Donna, UK

I work in a nursery and some of the comments are adorable. Here are some examples:-
Little boy: "When will your baby hatch?"
Little girl: (with massive freaked out eyes as she said it) "The baby is gonna get bigger and bigger and bigger until your head has to fall off, then your baby's head will come out."
Little boy: "I can hear your baby crying!"
Little twin girls: "Is your baby kicking?" If I say no they'll reply "Well mine is!"
Melanie, UK

Two weeks ago I was getting my three year old Son ready to go to the Ante-natal Clinic and he said "Mummy where are we going today?"
So I replied "to Ante-natal."
With a confused look on his little face he asked me "Mummy what does she look like? I haven't met her before, have I?"
Toni, UK

When I was pregnant with my Son, we got my Daughter who was two, one of the baby dolls that cries and wets like a real baby to get her used to the noise. She used the baby's bottle to 'feed' my tummy. She also used to push her mouth on my tummy and yell "Hi Brudder!" just to get him to kick her.
Jacqui, UK

When I was pregnant I came home from hospital after being kept in for a day, and my Son turned to me and said "Erm, Mummy, have they put the baby back in your tummy now?" He had been told that I would go into hospital and that's when the baby would come out so he assumed when I stayed for a day they had taken her out and then put her back in!
Laurie, UK

My Daughter (three years old) crawled into my bed the other morning and started rubbing my belly, then she said "Mommy can the baby come out today?"
When I said "No, she has to keep growing" my Daughter said "But if she grows bigger she'll break your belly!" It was so sweet, she seemed genuinely worried.
Krystal, USA

My 5 year old Daughter asked me the other day "Mommy, Why are you fat?" I said "Because your baby Brother is in my tummy."
To which she replied "But why's your butt fat? The baby can't be in your butt too!"

Thanks Hun!
Whitney, USA

I'm coming up to nine weeks pregnant and we (being my Parents and I) felt it was time to inform my younger Brothers (ages ten and eight) of what was going on.
So, we sat them down, and my Mom told them, "Well, you two are going to be Uncles." Of course, neither one of them understood, so she said, "Your Sister is having a baby."
The older of the two smiled and laughed, normal reaction. But, the youngest one had this terrified look on his face. My Mother asked him what was wrong, to which he replied, "I don't know how to be an Uncle! Can't he (the oldest) just be the Uncle?" We laughed and told him he didn't need to *do* anything to be an uncle, and then he said, "Yeah I do! I need to grow a moustache!"
So, now my eight year old Brother is working on growing his moustache, because that's what makes someone an Uncle. Ha Ha!
Mia, USA

My youngest Brother seems to think I'm just going to "Get really fat and then explode a baby out." Which, from what I understand, he's not far off!
Melanie, UK

My Little girl was on the bus with me one day and was looking at a pregnant lady sat near us.   She said "Mummy, why's that lady so fat?"

So I said "She has a baby in her tummy" to which she replied, "Mummy why she eat a baby?" It got most of the other Women on the bus laughing as my Daughter was not exactly quiet when she said it!
Kimberley, UK

My three year old has been shouting through my bellybutton "You can come out now we have put your cot up! Oh and I'm your big Sister!"
Lucy, UK

My Sister is due Christmas Day and she asked her three year old whether he is looking forward to the baby being here. He said "No" so my Sister asked "What are we going to do then when the baby is born?" He said "We will put it back!" Ha Ha!
Jess, UK

Conversation with my three year old Nephew:-
Me: "Look the baby is kicking Mummy's belly!"
Him: *looks at her belly and notices it moving* He gets up and wanders off into his bedroom.
Me: "Where you going?"
Him: *wanders back in with a toy hammer* "Hey baby! If you don't stop hitting my Mummy's belly I'm going to bash you big time!"
Chrissy, UK

When I put my Daughter to bed last night (she's three) she was talking about the baby and I asked her "Are you excited? It won't be long before he is here."
Then she went on to tell me "The baby will be born out of your mouth."
I was like "Erm no, the baby will come out of Mummy's belly" but she told me that no, she was certain the baby was going to come out of my mouth!
Lacey, UK

My Son makes me laugh every day, but today was one of those classics. I've been getting quite a lot of nosebleeds, normal pregnancy stuff. Today while I was getting him dressed, blood started to trickle down my nose a little and he asked "Mummy, why is your nose hurting you?" I wiped it and said "Don't worry, it's just all part of having your little baby Sister."
He stopped for a minute and then he asked "Will she be coming out of your nose?"
Lorna, UK

My Sister has twin boys, aged four and she is pregnant with another baby at the moment. She is due any time soon and so I asked them if they were excited they said "No" and I said "Well how is Mummy then?" They both replied at the same time "Really fat, can't even get your arms round her!" Then to make it even funnier they both held out their arms to show how big her belly was! Ha Ha!
Sarah, UK

My baby Sister was four during the time I was pregnant. She was always so worried about the baby because she is actually more like my Daughter than my Sister. I was eating a banana one day and I was really hungry so I was eating it really fast. Well my little Sister came up to me and said "Sis, slow down! The baby can't chew that big of bites she's gonna choke on it!" then rubbed my belly and said "That's ok baby I got after Mommy for you, you'll be ok!"
Marsha, USA

My four year old was the first to tell me I was pregnant, the one who insisted it was a girl (he was right) and now he wants to hug my tummy, and kiss 'the baby' all the time. He will crawl up on the couch and ask if he can lay his head on my belly. Once he did this and as soon as there was pressure, the baby kicked. He jumped back to ask what happened. I told him the baby kicked him, I was still laughing. He stared at me for a second, then back at my belly. He said "You shouldn't let the baby wear shoes in there." I love it!
Kirsty, USA

When I was pregnant with my Son, I was almost seven months gone and I was really into sushi (cooked rolls). We were at my favorite sushi place and we had just eaten dinner when a little girl came up to me. She stared at me for the longest time and then asked "Are you really full?" I tried so hard not to bust out laughing. I just smiled and said "Yes I am!"
Samantha, USA

I was standing in line at a grocery store and there was a Woman with a little boy standing behind me. She was pointing to my stomach and saying to her Son "Look there's a baby in there." He looked at me and then back at her in disbelief, then he pointed to my stomach and shouted "Baby!" His Mother said "Yes there's a baby in there." Then he walked over to a heavy set Man who was standing in front of me in line and he pointed at the Man's stomach and said "Baby?" It was hilarious! The Man in front of me took it very well, he just laughed.
Laura, USA

One day, I was with my family, and we were all talking about how the pregnancy was going. My two year old little Cousin looked at me and went "Where's the baby?" I told him it was in my tummy still. So he lifted up my shirt, in front of everyone, to look at my belly. He then told me that he didn't see it.
I said "Well, you can't see it yet because it's still inside my tummy."
His reply: "Make it come out then."
Jane, USA

I went to the Doctor for the first time last week. My five year old happened to be off school because she had to go to the Doctor for an ear infection. I had to take her with me to the Obstetrician. So I told her they were going to check my tummy to make sure the baby was doing okay. We got into the room and my Doctor decided we should just do a pap (vaginal scan) to get it out of the way since I was seven weeks at the time.

My Daughter was sitting in the chair beside me and they draped the cover over my knees. As they are starting to do the pap she looked at me with his horrible disgusted face and said "Mommy, eww this is gross! What are they doing?" Of course the Doctor and Nurse are laughing and I said "Honey, I told you they had to check Mommy's tummy" so she replied "Well I thought they were going to check from the *other* end!" It was so funny, everyone in the room was laughing hysterically!
Josie, USA

My Mom told me about when she was pregnant with my little Sister. We were out shopping and my Mom was in a dress. All of a sudden, I walked up to a stranger, lifted my Mom's skirt up over her tummy to show off "my baby". My Mom says that she was lucky she was wearing underwear that day, I'm just thinking I'm glad I don't remember!
Cherie, USA

During my last pregnancy I was driving my kindergartener to school and I had to pull over to throw up (morning sickness, yay!) I didn't want her to worry so when I got back in the truck I told her "It's ok sweetie. Sometimes when Mommies have babies in their tummies they feel a little sick."
The next day I went into her classroom to help out with reading time and her Teacher pulled me aside and surprised me by congratulating me on my new pregnancy and telling me that my Daughter had walked into the classroom and loudly announced that I had puked all over

the street and that "Mommy wouldn't get so sick if she'd stop eating all those babies." Ha Ha!
Julie, USA

I showed my six year old Son the DVD from my ultrasound and was pointing out the body parts of the baby. At one point he said "Wait! You mean the baby doesn't have any clothes on?" It cracked me up.
Mary, UK

My two and a half year old Son came up to me one morning and said "Momma look, baby tister in there eating her breakfast!" While pointing at my tummy. It was really sweet, his imagination is unreal.
Jacqui, USA

I am a part-time Nanny for a six year old girl and a couple weeks ago I was taking care of her, and since I hadn't had time to change after my baby shower I was wearing this cute little dress, which happened to show cleavage. So when I bent down to start painting with her, she said "Oh my gosh Summer, your boobies are so full of milk they're about to fall out!" She was so serious, and even though I tried to explain that since the baby isn't born yet, there's no milk, she kept insisting all night that there was!
Summer, USA

I had been trying to find a way to tell my three year old Son that I'm pregnant. I had a Sister in Law who was nearing the end of her pregnancy so I kept showing him

her belly saying, "There's a baby in there." Well he wouldn't believe me and then one day I asked him "Where's the baby?" He walked up to my boobs and said matter of fact, "There mommy, in boob." Ever since he has proceeded to tell everyone that babies come from boobs. Even to the point where one day my Husband was scratching his chest and my Son walked up to him and said, "Oh it's the baby huh?"
Shania, USA

Right now I'm twenty eight weeks pregnant with my second baby. My Son is six years old and he's beyond excited to get a baby Sister. So, he loves rubbing and kissing my belly and saying "Hi" to his Sister all the time, so, he gets that she's in there somewhere. However, we were sitting in bed the other night watching some TV before it was bedtime and a diet pill commercial comes on. He focuses in on it and once it was over he turned to me and said, "Mommy, you need to get some of those to deal with the extra weight and squishiness you've been going through." My Husband almost had a hernia and was doing his best to not laugh out loud. I guess my Son doesn't understand that Mommy has to put on some weight in order to have a healthy baby. So of course, my dear Husband decided to tell our Son that it would only get worse before it got better! Like Father like Son!
Cindy, USA

I have two younger brothers, and when my Mom was pregnant with the younger one, the older one was about six or seven. Anyway, Mom would always ask us to talk to the baby and he would always say "No." Now, this kid had a knack for deciding how things happened on his own. For instance, when Mom told him she was going to have a baby he asked when she and Dad would be getting married again (because he had figured that babies came from marriage). So one day Mom asked him to talk to the baby and he said, "Okay" and heaved a big sigh, he then proceeded to climb onto the couch, plug my Mother's nose and tilt her head back, opening her mouth. Then he spoke into her mouth because he figured that was the way to talk to the baby!

Jess, USA

I was nine weeks pregnant and had just recently told my two and a half year old Daughter. I walked into her room a couple of days later to clean it and she just lost it. She started crying because she thought the baby was going to take her toys and watch her TV. I explained to her that the baby wasn't big enough to do that yet but when the baby was big enough she should share anyway.
Normally when she wakes up she comes into my room and wakes me up. Well yesterday morning I felt something pushing against my mouth and something digging into my belly button. I opened my eyes and jumped up. My Daughter had a toy in each hand and was trying to shove them in my mouth and bellybutton. I asked "what are you doing?" She replied, "Well you said share, so I'm letting the baby play with my toys, so eat it!"

Marsha, USA

Every morning during the early stages of pregnancy I would wake up and have to go to the bathroom and be sick, and pee and whatever else. My two year old

Daughter would always be sleeping and didn't know that I was being sick. One morning I got up and I didn't hear her get out of bed behind me. I went into the bathroom and just waited for it all to come, as usual. I started throwing up and she came up beside me and started rubbing my back and saying "It's okay Mama, I'll take care of you." Another morning she decided that she wanted to try and get breakfast for herself while I was in the bathroom. I walked into the kitchen and there was milk and cereal everywhere! But somehow she had managed to get two bowls full of milk and cereal as well. She was sitting on the floor eating her cereal and looked at me and said "Mama, I got us breakfast." She patted the floor and says, "Sit down, eat!"
Marie, USA

My Daughter is almost potty trained, and she and my Partner were tickling each other and they decided to gang up on me and start tickling me. Well I was laughing so hard that I couldn't talk and I tried to get up because I really had to pee. I didn't quite make it and ended up slightly peeing myself. My Daughter looked at me and said, "Mommy, do you want to wear one of my pull-ups so you don't have another accident?" My partner and I cracked up laughing!
Jamie, USA

I used to babysit these two kids, and I ran into them at Wal-mart and was telling their Mom I was pregnant, and the little boy who was four looked up at me and said "Where is the baby?" I put his hand on my tummy and my baby kicked and he said "Oh my God! You ate her!

Mommy, Mommy help the baby she can't get out! I always knew you were crazy!" I laughed and we had to explain to him that babies grew inside their Mommy's tummy before they are born. It was hilarious, everybody at Wal-mart was peeking around corners of the aisles trying to figure out what was up!
Alison, New Jersey, USA

My Son is five years old, and he is starting to understand that Mommy has a baby in her belly. So we haven't had 'the birds and the bees' conversation yet and he asked me one night if I knew where babies came from, and I said "Yes, do you?"
He said "Yep, you have to drive to this baby factory that is very far away, then you look at the pictures of all the babies and decide which one you like best. then you got to have surgery cause they got to put the baby inside you, then you come home and wait for it to grow and then a long, long, long time goes by and you got to go to the hospital and they open your belly and take it back out and you get to take it home and play with it." I still don't know who told him this or whether he just tried to work it out for himself!
Lexie, USA

I was sitting down on the couch one evening with my twenty year old Brother and my four year old Son. My Son and I were having a conversation about how babies grow inside ladies bellies, and I said to my Son "You know you were once a little baby inside Mama's tummy." My Son replied with "Yeah then I grew bigger and bigger and I came out your mouth." My Brother and I just looked at each other and burst out laughing, it was so funny. The

next day we had to go to the Doctor's surgery for a check-up as I was pregnant again and my Son knows that I have another baby in my tummy. While we were sitting in the waiting room this Man walks in with a rather large beer belly and my son piped up with "Mama that Man has a baby in his belly too, just like you but his baby is bigger than your one." Oh my face turned bright red! Needless to say I had to share it with my Brother as soon as I finished my appointment and he thought it was hilarious too!
Stephanie, USA

I have a two year old Nephew and one day I asked him what my Son's name was going to be because I love the way he says the name I picked but he replied with "His name is Bob, well his real name is not Bob but I'm gonna call him Bob cause you don't always have to call someone their name, like you call me Bubba so I'm calling him Bob and don't try to tell me not to." Ha Ha!
Natasha, UK

At our twelve week ultrasound we took our eight year old Son along to meet his Brother or Sister who's living in my tummy. While staring at the monitor, seeing this weird-looking object twisting and twirling while Mommy and Daddy are going on about how big the baby has grown, out of the blue he said "I'm having a Sister." Mystified we asked him how he knew since it was too early to tell from the ultrasound and what would an eight year old boy know about such things? Without blinking he replied: "She does not have a penis. Look! There's nothing between her legs!" I almost died as the Doctor couldn't

look up, he was laughing too much. I explained that we wouldn't be able to see a penis just yet as the baby was too small!
Kerry, UK

I was sitting in the back seat of the car with my three year old Daughter, talking to her about how she's going to be a big Sister. I decided to ask her if she would like to go shopping with me for a toy for the baby. She said "Yeah I'm going to get the baby a toy but I have to wait till the baby comes out."
I said "Why do you have to wait?"
She said "The box won't fit in your belly so I have to wait."
So funny!
Cheryl, UK

That's all for this book, I hope you enjoyed reading! There are two more books in the 'Laugh Out Loud!' series:-

Laugh Out Loud! – Babies
Laugh Out Loud! – Kids

If you are leaving a review, thank you for your feedback! (you can write a review on the Amazon site or on goodreads)

You can find the Laugh Out Loud! Blog at http://laughoutloud-books.blogspot.co.uk/ where I am constantly adding new stories from my own family, especially comments from my little boy who makes me laugh every day!

I have also got a Facebook page dedicated to this series where you can add your own comments and stories at https://www.facebook.com/pages/Laugh-Out-Loud/420362314743645

Happy reading!
Sharon Irish